YOU
Wouldn't
LIKE IT
Here

A Guide to the *REAL*
Upper Peninsula of Michigan

Lon L. Emerick

From notes by Sam Satterly

with disturbing illustrations
by Carolyn Damstra

©2005 North Country Publishing

©2007 North Country Publishing & Avery Color Studios, Inc.

ISBN-13: 978-1-892384-43-0
ISBN-10: 1-892384-43-4

Library of Congress Control Number: 2005927154

First Edition 2005

10 9 8 7 6 5

Published by
Avery Color Studios, Inc.
Gwinn, Michigan 49841

Dedicated to Henry David Thoreau

"You must love the crust of the earth on which you
dwell more than the sweet crust of
any bread or cake."

AND TO

the Upper Peninsula residents who live in,
love, and protect this special land.

". . . and this place, which some would say is on the edge of nowhere, for me is the center of everywhere."

—Heather Lende
If You Lived Here, I'd Know Your Name
News from Small-Town Alaska

Contents

Illustrations

Prologue

At the end of the 2004 firearm deer-hunting season, I performed my usual survey and winterization of the deer blinds on our eighty-acre homestead. As I approached my most deluxe stand on the edge of a deep ravine I call Deer Valley, I was surprised to see faded human tracks in the snow. When I inspected the interior of the blind, it was clear that someone had spent considerable time sitting in the structure while I was occupied with other tasks.

Left behind in the blind were scribbled notes urging newcomers and tourists to stay away from the Upper Peninsula. In the interest of providing balance—since I have written lyrically about the charms of this region—I decided to assemble the intruder's thoughts into coherent form. Old professor that I am, I could not keep myself from accepting the writer's challenge and editing his polemic and colorful language for grammar, spelling and word choice.

I was unable to find a listing for a "Sam Satterly" in any area directory, so I assume it is a pen name. In hopes that a reader might recognize the trespasser's writing style, I present now his note to me exactly as he penned it.

Lon Emerick
Skandia, Michigan
September, 2005

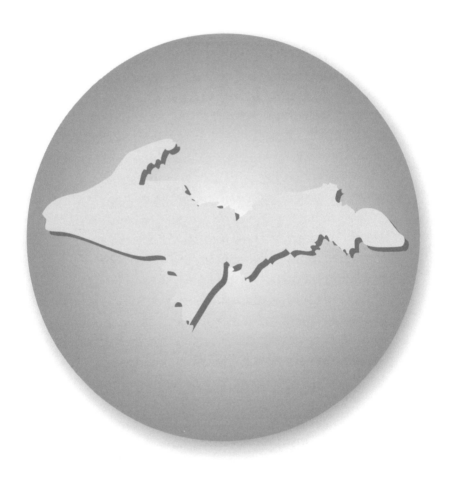

SAM
Satterly's
LETTER

Hey, Emerick,

I used this here blind on the first day of deer season. Pretty comfy, eh? Even a heater. Real fancy brass plate with your name on it—but what the heck is a "Taj Mahal?" Hope you don't mind. You wasn't here and it's a real nice spot looking down the valley.

I wandered around some on the way in here and came out in that field you have, with another deer stand up in the big hemlock tree.

Bet you think I wouldn't know what that wooden circle-thing you built was. But I saw it right off. A bunch of us Satterlys took a trip to Cornwall last year to find our "roots" and stopped by Stonehenge. So I knew what you built back there was a Woodhenge . . . didn't think a professor would be able to do that. Pretty good.

But I didn't see no deer from your blind. Not a hair even. So, I looked around for something to do and found your books about the U.P. They're pretty good, you know, but what's wrong with you? You make it sound like paradise here in the U.P. and that's just going to attract more of them trolls from down below. Or worse, people from other states, like on the West Coast. We don't want to be Californicated up here!

I found your little notebook where you write down stuff, this, that and the other thing. Looks to me like you are up to writing more dumb books to lure people to the U.P.

So, anyway, I decided to write my own book about why people wouldn't like it up here. I ain't much at writing so maybe you

can make something out of my scribbles.
I expect you won't do it though because
you seem determined to sing the praises
of our God's country.

Speaking of God's country, have you no
shame, Emerick? In one of these here
books you even drag the clergy in to try to
convince folks that the U.P. is a paradise.
Since I wasn't seeing no deer, anyway, only
red squirrels and chick-a-dees, I copied
that story here just like you wrote it down.
Maybe it will make you see what a dangerous
thing you're doing—inviting folks to fill up
and maybe tear up our U.P. Probably won't
do any good, though, just help me pass the
time here in your fancy deer blind.

> *My friends, Johnny and Alice*
> *Penhale of Negaunee took a*
> *trip around the world in their*
> *later years. On their world tour,*
> *the Penhales visited Catholic*
> *churches wherever they*
> *happened to be. In a church in*

Sidney, Australia, they saw a white phone on the wall. A small sign read, "Direct Line to God—calls $10,000." A church in Budapest had a similar phone and sign, but this time the call cost $8,000. In Paris, the cost was $4,000. Finally, in New York City, a phone call direct to God cost $2,000. Upon returning home to Negaunee, John visited a local church to see what a phone call to God would cost. A sign proclaimed that such a call would be 10¢. John sought out the priest and asked why a call from Negaunee was only 10¢ when it cost so much more to call God from places overseas and cities in the United States. The priest smiled and said, "Because from here, it's a local call."

Cause I had a lot of time with no deer coming by, I studied that map of the United States you have up on the wall by the window looking down over the valley and them deer trails. That's a great map. Gene Sinervo drew the U. P. just the way I think of it.

Emerick, you might be surprised to learn that me and the boys agree with those development folks who are pushing to make U.S. Highway 2 into a four-lane freeway from the Big Mac Bridge all the way to Ironwood. But we would build it with no off-ramps. Then them trolls from below the bridge could whiz along across the U.P. for 300 miles and not bother us at all. But you probably won't help us out with that, either. You're too busy writing them love letters to the U.P.

Anyway, thanks for the use of your deer blind. I didn't mess it up none.

Sam Satterly

The Official.. Map f Michigan

Drawn in Michigan's Upper Peninsula
By Eugene S. Sinervo ~ 1972 ©

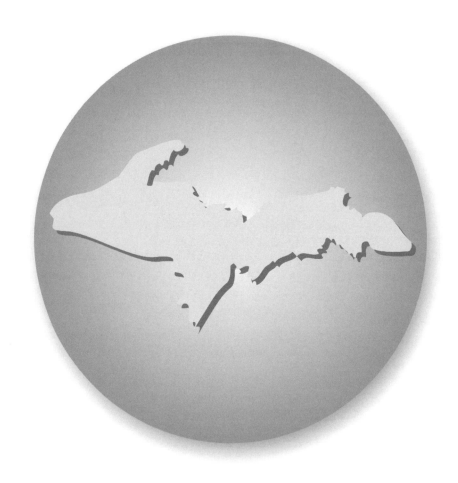

THE Real U.P.

YOU WOULDN'T LIKE IT HERE. The Upper Peninsula of Michigan is the ultimate Thule; the back of beyond; a vast wasteland; a worthless wilderness. As my city-raised Dad used to say, "It's miles and miles of nothing but miles and miles." Everything you have ever heard about the U.P. is either a pack of lies or a bunch of fantasies.

Not only are these fairy tales wrong-headed, they could be hazardous to unwitting visitors. It is one thing to have to live in this desolate and forbidding place— what I don't understand is why people would drive hundreds of miles to get here.

Are you getting the picture? I kid you not—the terrain is rocky and difficult, the

weather terrible, the wildlife unfriendly, the human residents weird and sometimes dangerous.

After all, this is the end of the road, so all kinds of characters fetch up here. The men even name their trucks! Pickups are adorned with signs—names like "Road Kill," "Mr. Wonderful" or "Crabby Dick." Only misfits or people in the witness protection program gravitate to this doleful region.

Visitors, beware!

Let me say it again for emphasis: Forget all those slick chamber of commerce brochures promising fun and fulfillment in the far north. This dismal land brings out the worst in people, though they often cover it with sick humor.

Consider this typical Upper Peninsula ending of an anniversary celebration that took place this past summer:

Elmer and Gladys Trelawny
celebrated their 50th wedding

anniversary with a sit-down dinner for ninety-seven guests at the Chenoweth Bar and Grill in the small village of Dismal Seepage. Champagne flowed and toasts were made by several relatives and close friends. Gladys was the last to speak. She raised her glass and began: "I've been married to this man for fifty years," she said, pointing at Elmer. A long pause ensued. "And if I had killed him when I wanted to, I'd be out of jail by now."

Geography

YOU DON'T NEED TO KNOW much about geography to appreciate the fact that the Upper Peninsula of Michigan is in the north. The very, very far north.

Here are the facts: Marquette, the largest "city" and nominal capital of the U.P. (with a population of 21,000—now doesn't that tell you something about this remote region?) is located 150 miles north of the 45th parallel. For crying out loud, Quebec City is farther south!

We do have lots and lots of rocks and trees up here. The rugged ankle-breaking granite is everywhere. And the forests are so thick that tourists get lost all the time. Hunters even find their bones years later.

Not worried about getting lost because you are strolling on an obvious trail? Well, keep in mind that mountain bikers, ATV

You Wouldn't Like It Here

riders and snowmobilers by the hundreds race through the woods up here and are not likely to slow down for anyone or anything.

Oh, and this should give you chills about coming up here—we have more than a hundred ghost towns in the U.P. The people who are alive left long ago. Most of these old towns are haunted by the restless ghosts of miners killed in the copper and iron mines. The old mine shafts are abandoned and filled with water now and the upper levels are home to thousands of bats. One slip into the dark water or one bite from a rabid bat and you are gone forever.

Seems like a mighty big risk to take a vacation. Doesn't it make sense to go to Disney Land instead?

The little kids in the U.P. know that fun is not found in this frigid wasteland—at least they do until about age six when the local genetic torpor sets in. The other day, Sarah Satterly, my three-year-old granddaughter,

crawled up in my lap and asked if I could make a noise like a frog.

"Sure," I said, and then asked, "Why do you want me to sound like a frog?"

"Cause," she replied. "Mom said that when you croak we get to go to Disney Land."

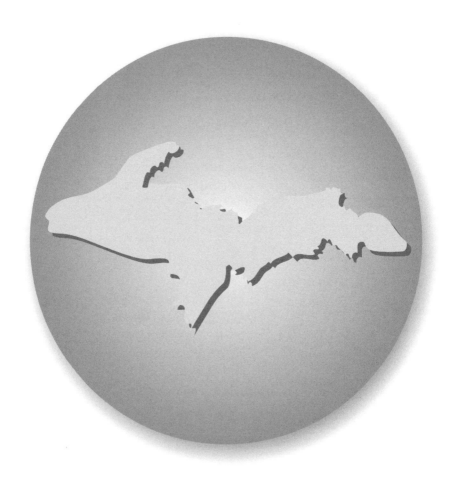

Climate

WE DON'T HAVE A CLIMATE in the U.P—
we have weather. Do we ever have weather!
There are only two seasons up here in the
sticks: Endless winter and about four weeks
of mud, bugs and visitors. If you seek a
polar climate, have a need to make yourself
miserable or if you need to atone for a life
of sin, then maybe you're a candidate for
our glacier-land.

Let me tell you about the snow. Some
parts of the Upper Peninsula get as much
as 300 inches of the white stuff—in one
winter. And it doesn't melt all winter. That
very same snowflake that fell on September
27 is still there under a huge drift on April
27. Maybe even May 17.

Residents find all kinds of ways to cope
with the snow that falls and falls and piles

and piles. Regular shovels are hard on the back and not very efficient at moving the drifts.

So some Yooper way back invented what we call a "snow scoop." Made out of metal, it's a giant version of the sand scoops kids use on the beach. One winter, my neighbor Walt Skewis got so tired of the snow he threatened to tie his snow scoop on the top of his old pickup truck and just start driving south. "When someone asks what that strange contraption is on top of my truck," Walt said, "I'll know I've gone far enough and can settle down."

We also have to worry about the weight of the snow on the roofs of our houses and camps. Some residents climb up on the roof and use their snow scoop to push the snow over the edge. Of course, every winter some home and camp owners go right over the edge along with their snow scoop.

One clever invention for clearing roofs of snow build-up is the "roof rake," where the unfortunate resident can stand on the ground, reach up to the roof with the very long "rake" and pull the snow down . . . all over him.

One unusually heavy-snow winter, I was grousing to my mother-in-law (which was a switch, 'cause she was usually grousing about *me*) that I was tired of raking roofs— my home, my garage, the woodshed, our old camp on Lake Superior. I guess I was looking for some sympathy. She responded in her usual understanding way, with a comment that has become part of our family lore: "Well, your problem is that you just have too many roofs!"

When I told my cousin George Satterly, who has always lived in Florida and has no knowledge of, or interest in, the north coun- try, that I was raking my roof for the fourth time in a month, he was puzzled. "I didn't know you had thatched roofs in the U.P."

We have so much snow that it causes the locals to go bonkers every year. Bad weather takes on moral implications—the interminable white season is our cross to bear. A clear, warm day is greeted with alarm: There will be some terrible climatic calamity in payback for the brief respite. "We're going to pay for this later," old-timers utter, in tones of conviction and resignation.

And it gets even weirder. One building contractor, Alex Trezona, seriously pro-posed using snow as fill on a construction job he was doing. Now, it's true that this discussion took place after several rounds of drinks at Old Joe's bar late one frigid February evening. At that time, the snow banks around Old Joe's parking lot were more than eleven feet high.

Insects

THEN, WHEN THE SNOW FINALLY MELTS,
guess what form of animal life bursts forth
in astounding profusion? Right, bugs!
Would you believe that snow fleas emerge
in dense clouds even before the snow is
gone?

But the "real" bug season extends from
May to September and features several
relentless insects, in overlapping hordes.
Here are four insect pests just waiting to
feast on our visitors:

First come the *blackflies*. These are
small, pesky critters, seemingly undeterred
by insect repellent. Blackflies travel in
dense swarms and like wet areas such as
creeks and rivers. We have lots of water in
the U.P. Remember all that snow? Blackflies
are masters at sneaking under collars and

up pant legs to invade private parts of your anatomy. They especially like to probe around eyes and ears. Before you know it, the little devils have opened a hole in your skin, injected an anticoagulant and siphoned off a snootful of your blood. You are left with a painful irritation and swelling. My neighbor, George Penhale, says that a blackfly bite works better than Botox for eliminating wrinkles. Cheaper, too.

So if you don't mind donating some of your DNA, come up and play with the blackflies in May and June.

Wood ticks, the most evil of all our pests, lead the second assault wave. You find them in grassy areas and mixed woodlands. Rather, they find you. Wood ticks are very, very, stealthy—they jump on your clothes when you walk through fields and forests and then crawl in next to your warm skin.

Actually, wood ticks are not insects. They have eight legs—all the better to explore your body—and are members of the spider family. Arachnophobia!

Ticks burrow into any tender spot they can find and proceed to suck your blood. They are hard to detect because they don't buzz or whine when they make contact. With their hard shell-like bodies and strong mouthparts, they are almost impossible to pluck off once they have dug into your skin. When you do manage to pull a tick out of its dining site, its tenacious mouthparts often are left in your skin. This can create really nice infections, to say nothing of other dread disease possibilities.

It is better to stay away from the U.P. during May, June and most of July rather than risk an encounter with wood ticks.

Even the rest of the year can be a problem. One May, I put a strip of Scotch tape over a tick on the windowsill of my hunting camp. When I opened the old shack in October and removed the tape, the little bugger walked away!

You wish to know all about our *mosquitoes*? Well, ignore all the scary legends

about these bloodsuckers in the Upper Peninsula. We don't have a single mosquito up here: They are all married and have thousands of children.

There is no need to tell you any more horror stories about our resident mosquitoes except to say that they are so large they can stand flat-footed and mate with a full-grown turkey. At least that's what I've heard. Never actually saw it myself.

So, when the blackflies have finished their reproductive cycle, when wood ticks become dormant, when the mosquitoes have waned to nearly tolerable levels, a new flying pest, the dreaded *deer fly* arrives. It also wants some of your blood and is not deterred by *anything*. The only way to stop a deer fly from biting is to kill it. Then five more come to attend the funeral.

But, you say, there is insect repellent which will thwart these malevolent bugs. Yes, visitor, there are some kinds of very strong bug dope you can use which may provide limited relief. However, in an hour or two after you apply it to your exposed skin, the toxic ingredients can be measured in your liver. Maybe that is another reason why the local population is so unstable.

Wildlife

ONE OF THE BIGGEST SCAMS used to lure visitors to the U.P. is the opportunity to watch wildlife: Come north and see the beautiful whitetail deer, awesome black bear and elusive moose.

Well, I must warn you: The wildlife up here is dangerous.

We have more *deer* in the Upper Peninsula than humans and many of them are determined to commit suicide in the grill of your SUV. A deer gets special recognition from its peers if it manages to careen through the windshield and take you out, too. Then there is the costly damage to your vehicle and the inevitable delays while you try to coax a mechanically challenged local repairman to get you back on the road and out of this Godforsaken wilderness.

It's something to think about if you ignore my warning and drive on the narrow roads with dense forests on both sides. Which pretty much describes all the roads in this benighted region.

Now, if you do decide to venture into the woods on foot, be aware that *bears* will be expecting you. They lurk about in the thickets just waiting for an unwary hiker with food in his pack or even a casual walker foolish enough to carry a Snickers bar in his pocket.

You are thinking I exaggerate. After all, I'm just a backwoods guy and I'm probably making up bear stories just to discourage you from visiting.

Would you pay attention to opinions from the Army Corps of Engineers? The Corps has established test wells to monitor leftover toxins and water quality all through an area surrounding a former air force base.

My friend, Lizzie Kernow, is in charge of the contract for the annual testing. Last year, the Corps guys showed up right on time, and she took them out in the woods to locate the wellheads. Most are within sight or sound of paved roads, housing developments or airport runways.

The guys took one look at the wooded paths they would have to walk in to get to the wells and said, "No way. We are not going in those woods—there might be BEARS in those woods."

So don't come to me if you get mugged by a bear in a U.P. forest.

There are plenty of other wild animals that live up here in the boonies and they all take pleasure in bedeviling tourists and newcomers.

Here's just a sampling: *Porcupines* love to chew on your car's brake lines to get high on the hydraulic fluid. You may not realize what has happened to your brakes until you are careening out of control down Quincy Hill into Hancock. *Raccoons* are all over the place just waiting to jump into the garbage can by your campsite or take a

bite out of your children. They also fight each other during the darkest part of the night; that's a sound that can lift you straight up out of your cabin cot or sleeping bag. And *skunks*, well, you know what they are good at.

THE Local RESIDENTS

BE WARNED! If you travel to the Upper Peninsula, be cautious of the residents. Keep your car locked at all times and when entering a building, always locate the nearest exit. We are not happy bumpkins up here in the north. We have our own brand of misery from being cold and isolated too long.

You probably have heard about those kooky people who have themselves put in deep freeze when they die; they hope to be thawed out at some future date and live again. What you may not know is that they experimented in the U.P. long ago to see how far they could chill people and not kill them. Behold the Yooper!

Just beneath the skin of every Yooper is a layer of permafrost; the ice chills all normal human attributes. The technical medical diagnosis for this condition is hypothermia of the spirit. The local residents have never really gotten warm.

The typical Yooper is torpid and tight-lipped. It comes from the effects of isolation, chronic agony and inbreeding. Over the years, local residents have evolved in odd ways. They settled here because they could go no further.

We are suspicious of outsiders. Why do they want to come here when we know very well how miserable it is? Are they fools? Are they coming to view us quaint local yokels, have some laughs and then go home and tell jokes about the primitive life forms in the far north?

Don't try to get to know the locals. After all, we know that visitors, after leaving this country, will return to warmer climes and stimulating cities, and look forward to good, balanced meals that don't involve pasties* and venison.

On the very rare occasions when Yoopers do talk to visitors, you probably won't understand what they are saying, anyway. The melody pattern of their speech has strange up and down swoops. They substitute d and t for th sounds: "Dis, dat and the udder ting," a frequently uttered all-purpose phrase, means "This, that and the other thing."

An emphatic "hey" or "eh" is added at the end of most every utterance; it is more a challenge than a question.

Most disturbing of all is a strange inhaled "Yeehup" when silent intervals occur in the conversation; they occur often.

*A pasty (rhymes with nasty, if you want to sound like a local) is a meat and veg-etable pie. It's probably best not to ask about the specific ingredients—remember the old maxim: Don't ask the question if you don't want to hear the answer!

Anthropologists don't know if these quasi-verbal manifestations are affirmations, expressions of disgust, or symptoms of a rare respiratory illness caused by breathing mine dust, tree pollen and too much cold air.

So, how *should* one interact with Yoopers? It's best not to interact at all if you can avoid it. We settled here in the far north long ago because no one else wanted it; we revel in our distinctive way of life and wish to be left alone.

It's best to simply do the typical tourist things: buy a small pillow filled with balsam needles; eat a pasty (be sure to pronounce it "paste-ee"); get a souvenir baseball cap with a deer turd encased in plastic on the brim; and spend most of your time indoors at the casino.

Don't try to buy gas, order a meal or find a motel room on November 15, or the last Saturday in April. Those are High Holy Days—the opening of deer hunting season and the start of trout fishing season—and

U.P. National Holidays.

Whatever you do, don't try to fit in with the locals. We resent it; we think you are patronizing us because we know what wretched lives we lead.

Don't tell any jokes about poaching deer, eating road kill or things you have observed which prove that Yoopers are examples of evolutionary cul-de-sacs. In some circles, it's also best not to mention the movie *Escanaba in Da Moonlight.*

It's better to ask dumb questions because it gives us a little rush to feel superior.

Ask questions like:

"Have you lived here all your life?" There will be a long pause—then a laconic Yooper response: "Not yet."

Ask for directions—one of the rare pleasures we have is getting visitors lost in the vast forests.

Old Eddie Uren is a master at getting tourists lost. He seems so deliberate and sincere when he gives elaborate instructions how to get to a particular location, right down to telling his victims to look for the dead elm tree with a patch of moss on the north side. His favorite place to send people is off to the Sands Plains where it is very easy to get confused and disoriented by the web of woods roads radiating in all directions.

But Eddie always ends his complex directions with a wave of his arm and a caveat that tourists never hear correctly. As a visitor returns to his car, Eddie calls out after him, "You can miss it!"

Ask about using an outhouse. That question can lead to all sorts of fun for the locals.

My Uncle Bill Rosemergy is held in regional awe for the most outrageous outhouse stunt. Before an elderly maiden relative from Detroit came to visit, Bill, an electrician by trade, wired his outhouse. He installed a speaker under the seat platform and a remote control microphone in his cabin. Aunt Lucille delayed using the outdoor facility until she could wait no longer. Just when she got nicely settled down on the seat, Uncle Bill turned on the speaker and said, "Hey, lady, I'm working down here. You're blocking my light!"

I read somewhere that 97% of U.P. households have one or more television sets, but only 89% have indoor plumbing. Does this mean that there is more crap coming into the homes than is going out?

Under no circumstances should you ask questions like these:

"Where can I find a good blueberry patch?"

"Where can I fish for brook trout?"

"Where's a good spot to pick mushrooms?"

Almost without exception, a resident will stare at you for a minute or so—one of the rare times a Yooper makes eye contact—and then reply, "I could tell you, but then I'd have to kill you." He may smile a bit when he says it, but he is "dead" serious.

Although the men are invariably ominous,

visitors should be wary of U.P. women, particularly the older ones. Yooper men are so cold and phlegmatic that they rarely express affection to their women.

The other day, I was in the Eagle River General Store and overheard several good old boys solving the world's problems while they had their morning coffee. When one man was asked how his wife was doing, he replied, "You know, I love her so much that the other day I almost told her." Another man thumped the table and declared, "Lena, she is always asking me if I love her. Well, one day I got tired of her asking me that, so I said that I told her I loved her when we got married in 1958, and if I change my mind, I'll let her know."

One elderly woman, a resident of Misery Bay, is a legend among tourists in the Copper Country. Eliza Chegwidden makes sure to greet every tour bus stopping on the Keweenaw Peninsula and scope out the men. When she finds a guy without a female partner, she sidles up real close to him and announces, "You look just like my third husband." And it always works. The confused visitor, not knowing what to make of Eliza's comment, invariably asks, "How many husbands have you had?" Eliza then leans in even closer and replies, "Two."

That's regarded as a very sophisticated pick-up line in these parts.

We do take perverse pleasure in poking fun at tourists, especially those fussy visitors who want things like espresso and hummus.

My friend, Wesley Ollila (he's a Finn and the Satterlys are Cornish through and through, but he's a good guy), is a great storyteller and used to make the most marvelous wooden sleighs. He had to give up the work because of his health, but he still tells a great story. He's proud of helping start up the annual Aura Music Jamboree. Each July hundreds of people come to Aura to hear folk, country and traditional Finnish music. I almost have to stop mak-ing fun of U.P. festivals when I think about the Aura Music Jamboree. Since the park grounds and township hall where the festival occurs are right next door to the Ollila home, Wesley helps out at the event any way he can. He tells me a story about a fancy lady visitor and the traditional offering of bean soup. He has trouble getting out the whole story, 'cause he's laughing so hard still. That gets me laughing, too.

> *"Every year we make a really big batch of bean soup for the guests—we use a fifty-five-gallon drum. To stir the soup, we use a canoe paddle. So, this one lady, really dressed up she was and a bit snooty, you know, came up and watched our operation for a while. Seems like she couldn't decide whether to take a chance and buy a bowl of soup or not. She asked a bunch of questions. Finally, someone gave her a*

little cup of the soup to taste
and she keeps poking around
in it with a spoon. Well, she
took a sip or two, and right
then, I decide to have some
fun. So, I say to my buddy
kinda loud like, 'Hey, I know
what happened to that chip-
munk that was around here
begging for food—he's in the
soup!' Now that old gal, she
spit out a mouthful of bean
soup, dropped the cup and
hightailed it outta here!"

You've got to watch the locals all the time. Even serious issues like health and hospitals bring out the perverse U.P. humor:

I promised Danny Trevarton that I would never tell anyone this story about his famous practical joke. But what the heck, Danny went off to medical school, changed his name to D. Lawrence Trevarton, M.D., and is a plastic surgeon in Tampa.

Dr. Trevarton, as he insists even his old buddies must call him, came up to the U.P. only once in the last ten years. And then he turned folks off with his haughty manner, perfect teeth and impatient demands for latte and spinach quiche.

Anyway, back in the days when he was still a Yooper, he worked as an orderly during the summers of his pre-med college years. Assigned to the midnight shift in the emergency room, he found himself either bored by inactivity or up to his armpits in blood and bandages.

One particular night in August he was so bored he decided to liven up the hospital. Remembering that a new, inexperienced young woman had been hired as the receptionist in the central office, Danny called her and told her to page "Dr. Harry Scrotum."

Danny-boy hid in an examining room and watched. After three announcements were broadcast throughout the hospital calling *Dr. Harry Scrotum*, the charge nurse erupted from her desk, shouting, "Harry

Scrotum, Harry SCROTUM?" By then, the entire hospital staff was convulsed with laughter.

The memory of this bit of late night M*A*S*H humor lasted for almost a decade in the hospital legends. But never, at least till now, has the legend been connected to old Danny. Or should I say D. Lawrence Trevarton, M.D.?

FINDING
A Place
TO STAY

IT'S IN YOUR BEST INTEREST to keep driving—all night if you have to—and aim for Wisconsin or Minnesota. Ignore my advice and here is what you are likely to find:

> *An ancient resort named Dew Drop Inn or Black Bear's Rest. It will be owned and operated by Gloria and Floyd Gertz, disgruntled expatriates from a suburb of Detroit. The Gertzs believed the myth about the idyllic land "up north" and sank all their 401k money into a run-down cabin court on a shallow,*

weedy inland lake.

Now, Floyd and Gloria are trapped with an aging resort and spend their retirement days unplugging leaky toilets, washing sheets and fielding complaints from people like you who expect to find all the amenities of modern life. Conveniences like dishes, toilet paper, hot water and window screens. The Gertzs own a huge Rottweiler named Max that, when not slobbering on your shoes or knocking down your children, growls menacingly whenever you open the creaky door to your 1930s vintage cabin.

Don't risk it—keep on driving.

Entertainment

WELL, IF IT WERE ENTERTAINMENT you were after, you should have gone to Wisconsin Dells, the Henry Ford Museum, or considered checking yourself into a large downstate hospital for any elective procedure rather than coming to the Upper Peninsula. But, since you may already be here, let me tell you what passes for culture and entertainment in these parts:

There are some *museums*. They are all located in dark and dreary old buildings and staffed by terminally bored senior citizens. These museums will display graphic evidence of prolonged suffering:

- bones of tourists who ate two pasties for dinner
- bones of visitors who asked a resident to take them to a favorite blueberry patch

■ bones of residents and tourists lost in the deep woods and eaten by wild animals.

On the other hand, you could attend one of our local *festivals*, such as:

■ a pasty-throwing contest
■ a pasty-eating contest
■ a rock-skipping contest

A real favorite among local residents is the annual outhouse race. Imagine teams of grown men and women pushing decorated outdoor potties down through the icy streets of a small town. If you can't quite imagine that, think about the hundreds of deranged residents who come out and line the street to watch this spectacle.

Do you understand now why I refer to the U.P. as a theme park for the desperate and culturally challenged? It can be a mistake of grave consequence to even drive by the site of one of these disturbing festivals. Why, you might get caught up in the spirit and end up pushing (or riding in) the winning outdoor potty.

One of the tricks those dedicated folks at the tourist bureaus do to entice people to visit the Upper Peninsula is promoting the opportunity for *water sports*. The colorful brochures show happy families boating, fishing, kayaking, water skiing, windsurfing, swimming and just lying about on the beaches.

While it's true that the U.P. is surrounded by three beautiful Great Lakes, has hundreds of inland lakes and miles of sparkling streams, much of the year they are covered with ice and snow.

That may explain why *ice fishing* is so popular—what else is there to do? It's an exciting sport. You sit for hours in a cold, dark shack watching a dark hole cut in the ice.

Frank Pollack didn't quite get the objective of ice fishing. When he proudly brought home his big catch, his wife Helmi, although somewhat dubious, tried to fry up Frank's prize. Telling it later to her quilting

circle, Helmi said, "Frank went ice-fishing… he caught a big one. When I tried to fry it up on the stove, it darn near flooded my kitchen!"

And all year round our waters are home to dangerous creatures like polar bears, elephant seals, packs of wolves and, some say, sea monsters in the deepest waters.

What about the U.P. *nightlife*? To say that evenings are dull up here in the far north is another redundancy. The local idea of a fun time is a seven-course meal: A pasty and a six-pack of beer. Then turn on the black and white television set with the rabbit-ears antenna and watch Lawrence Welk re-runs. Finally, retire to a straw mattress, wrap up in coarse woolen blankets and try to survive the night.

There are some seedy taverns you might visit. In most every case, the bars up here are overheated, dimly-lit and smell of stale beer and other odors wafting from the back room. The bartender will be a tall, thin character named Leon with long, grimy hair and a tattoo on his right bicep proclaiming "Death before Dishonor." On the wall behind the bar is a large mural depicting Custer's Last Stand and a bumper sticker proclaiming *To take away my deer rifle, you will have to pry it from my cold, dead hands.*

A trio of beefy locals with substantial beer bellies will be perched on stools at the bar. They will be muttering darkly about the Dee-En-Are (Michigan Department of Natural Resources), United Nations Black Helicopters and timber wolves killing all their deer. Because their jeans are buckled so low on their ample hips, when they lean forward to put out a cigarette or fill up a glass, their sweatshirts ride up, revealing a disturbing amount of buttock cleavage. Locally, this is called "crack."

Intermittently the men will emit unexpected ejaculations such as, "Holy Waugh!" or "Yah, sure, you betcha."

When you enter, all conversation will stop and all heads will swivel to see just what foreigners have invaded their space.

There will be an ominous pause while they look over your L.L. Bean waffle-stompers and clean hiking pants with all the pockets; then the muttering will take on a disquieting tone. You won't quite be able to hear it, but this is what they are saying:

"What do them trolls want? Are they gonna move here and put up *No Trespassing* signs on our favorite hunting spots? Soon, they'll be whining that their fancy cell phones don't work this far north and the shopping malls are too small."

Leon drifts over to where the locals are growling and reminds them to "take it easy, guys. Remember, they're not just trolls from below the bridge, what they really are is *income*."

Don't you think it would be better for you to have a chicken dinner in Frankenmuth or a slice of cherry pie in Traverse City?

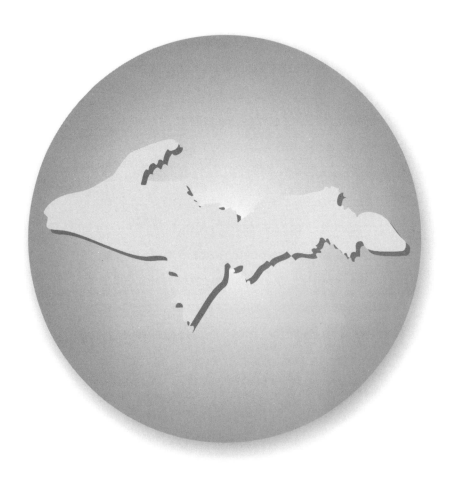

Epilogue

AS A LONG-TIME LOVER of this wondrous Superior Peninsula, I can appreciate Sam Satterly's concerns about what the future may bring to the region. Putting aside all the hyperbole and humorous attempts to scare off visitors or prospective immigrants, I offer only this plea:

> *Please don't come to the Upper Peninsula and try to alter the land or our way of life. Don't set about to change this place into the place you have just left (or fled).*

> *It is what it is and we like it that way.*

> *Rather, approach our beloved north country with reverence and awe.*

> *Fold yourself in here and let the land change you.*

ABOUT THE
Author

LON EMERICK was raised in a suburb of Detroit and exposed to education at Dondero High School and Michigan State University.

He fled the lower reaches of Michigan when he met and married a gal from the Upper Peninsula. As a result of severe stuttering and later recovery, he became a professor of speech pathology, teaching at "institutions" in West Virginia, Minnesota and Arizona, with the longest and most satisfying years at Northern Michigan University in Marquette.

Although he is the author of many professional textbooks and articles in speech pathology, he is pleased to be most identified with his later books about his adopted land— the Upper Peninsula of Michigan.

Lon Emerick lives now with his wife Lynn in a log home in the woods of West Branch Township, and spends many days exploring the woods and waters of which he writes.

CREDITS AND
Acknowledgements

The author and publisher acknowledge, with special thanks, permissions granted for use of original images, photographs and writings.

Front cover photograph: *End of Earth*. Adapted from a sign and photograph created by John A. Marchesi and Tim Cocciolone. © John A. Marchesi, 1985. Used by permission.

Map of the Real U.P. created by Eugene Sinervo © Eugene S. Sinervo, 1972. Used by permission: Vincent Sinervo

Back cover photos: Lynn McGlothlin
Top: Author Lon Emerick with Sam Satterly's notes at Taj Mahal hunting blind
Bottom: Woodhenge in an autumn field

The dedication quote by Henry David Thoreau is from *Walking*. Harper-Collins, 1994

The quote by Heather Lende, from *If You Lived Here, I'd Know Your Name* © Heather Lende, is reprinted by permission of Algonquin Books of Chapel Hill.

For the concept of "disturbing illustrations"— *Uncle Mike's Guide to the Real Oregon Coast* by Mike Burgess, illustrated by Steve McLeod. Left Coast Group, no date.

Lon Emerick books available from North Country Publishing:
(including those which so distressed Sam Satterly)

The Superior Peninsula: Seasons in the Upper Peninsula of Michigan
Merit award winner
Midwest Publishers Association

Going Back to Central: On the Road in Search of the Past in Michigan's Upper Peninsula
A Library of Michigan Notable Book

Best in Travel Books,
Midwest Publishers Association

Sharing the Journey: Lessons from my Students and Clients with Tangled Tongues

North Country Publishing
355 Heidtman Road, Skandia, MI 49885
email: northco@up.net
www.northcountrypublishing.com
Toll-free: 1-866-942-7898